Coaching Elementary Soccer

The easy, fun way to coach soccer for 6-year-olds, 7-year-olds, 8-year-olds, 9-year-olds, and 10-year-olds (kindergarten, first-grade, second-grade, and third-grade children)

Bryan Gilmer

This book is offered as a way to help adults think about coaching kids soccer. It reflects the author's opinions and is for educational purposes only. Readers should use caution and good judgment and make their own decisions, as they are responsible for ensuring their personal safety and the safety of their own team. Coaches should follow league rules and guidelines at all times. Children's names in the text, except for the author's son Quinn, are fictitious to protect the privacy of children coached. Neither Hillandale Sports Association nor Triangle United Sports Association authorized this book nor contributed to it, and all views expressed are solely those of the author.

Copyright © 2015 by Bryan Gilmer

All rights reserved.
Independently published in the United States as a Laurel Bluff Book.
bryangilmer.com

Gilmer, Bryan, 1972–
The easy, fun way to teach coach soccer for 6-year-olds, 7-year-olds, 8-year-olds, 9-year-olds, and 10-year-olds (kindergarten, first-grade, second-grade, and third-grade children)

Printed in the United States of America

10 9 8 7 6 5 4 3 2 1

ISBN 978-0983424833 (pbk)

First Edition

For Quinn, again and always

Contents

1. THE ROOTS OF MY APPROACH TO COACHING KIDS, P. 1

2. THE ESSENCE OF ELEMENTARY SOCCER, P. 5

3. BRYAN'S ELEMENTARY PRINCIPLES, P. 9

4. THE DISCIPLINES OF PRACTICE MIRROR THE GAME, P. 15

5. NO MORE BUNCH BALL, P. 21

6. THE MASTER STRATEGIES, P. 27

7. POSITION-SPECIFIC STRATEGIES, P. 39

8. STRATEGIES FOR SPECIAL SITUATIONS, P. 47

9. YOUR BEST TOOL: THE TEACHING SCRIMMAGE, P. 53

10. TAKE IT ONE THING AT A TIME, P. 57

   APPENDIX: TEAM MANAGEMENT, P. 59

1

The roots of my approach to coaching kids

Hi, I'm Bryan Gilmer. Quinn's dad.

Quinn's 8. He started playing when he was 4. I started as a rookie coach of his second team when I was concerned that his first – very nice – coach wasn't engaging the kids at the developmental stage where they were. That was in a purely recreational league. Now, we've advanced into a developmental league with two practices a week for more serious players. Through these experiences, he's developed solid soccer skills and learned a lot about how to play, and he really, really loves the game.

Like most youth soccer coaches, I learned on the job. As I have tagged along with Quinn, I've developed my own youth soccer coaching approach, with the fundamental principles of meeting the kids developmentally where they are and giving them real soccer strategies and skills in a logical sequence, one at a time, just as they are ready to master them.

I've learned how to help kids gain and develop these skills, to see success using them in games, and to have a ton of fun at the same time. I've been pleased to have the chance to share my approach to coaching preschoolers with hundreds of other volunteer parent coaches to help them get started or to coach more effectively. I detailed this approach in my first coaching book, *Coaching Little Kid Soccer.*

Now, I'm ready to share how I coach soccer players in the lower elementary grades. It's a quite a bit more involved, but even if you have never coached before, this book will show you how to get started as a rookie coach at the kindergarten, first-, second-, and third-grade levels. Of course, it will also help you build on any experience you have coaching little kid soccer and to take your coaching and your team's play to the next level.

In *Coaching Little Kid Soccer,* I pointed out that the pre-elementary game isn't much more complicated than arcade air hockey. The elementary game is certainly a bit more complex than that – but listen, it is still *way* simpler than the high school or professional game. Any kind, supportive, semi-organized parent can coach it very capably.

There are two main mistakes to avoid:

Avoid failing to teach and coach. You can't simply put the players onto the field and let them do what they will. They'll tend to bunch together and all follow the ball around the field like they did when they were 5. They will get in each other's way and lose to teams employing even a rudimentary strategy. They're ready for much more sophisticated soccer than that – but need to be showed how to do it one element at a time.

Avoid making the game overly or too-quickly complex at this age. This, of course, would be the opposite mistake. Elementary soccer is *way* simpler than many coaches – especially those who are or were accomplished high school, college, or adult soccer players themselves – try to make it. These coaches, with their experience in complicated frameworks and set plays, often shout cryptic directions in soccer speak ("Man on!" "Check back!" "Lay off for him!") that they've never explained to the kids. And the kids don't understand them! These coaches try to give their players six strategic concepts all at once, and the players get bewildered. They know they are failing, but they don't see why or know how to fix it. These coaches often insist they are preparing their players to compete down the road at those higher levels. But my experience is that they're failing them now by rushing players, being overly rigid and critical, setting unrealistic expectations, and, by their hyper-seriousness, taking the fun out of the game.

Imposing a more complex system of play or calling for more difficult decisions and actions than the players are able to accomplish causes confusion, anxiety, and stress for everyone. Guess what? That's not good leadership. It's not the way to win games, either. But I've heard many such coaches say they don't mind losing a lot of games now because what the players are learning is really important and will prepare them for later.

Sorry, but no! Kids who lose every game aren't going to stick with soccer long enough for any promise of future success to pay off.

If you are an effective coach, your team will play competitively each week and win a good number of games now. The object of the game of soccer is to score more goals than the other side and to win. The right strategy for a particular age of kid enables them to work together to accomplish that goal – this season. The kids know this and want to do it. Kids need to see their work and learning in practice pay off.

Now, hold on. I absolutely do prioritize player development above winning games. That means I'll play my weakest offensive player on offense for part of the game, even though it places us at a disadvantage, so he can have that experience and improve those skills. I'll sub out my best overall player for a rest break just like every other player, even if she's not tired – and especially when she's scored all our goals that day. Every child on the team will play substantial minutes in every game and play every position on the field during the season.

But you know what? I also begin games with our strongest lineup on the field to get us off to a great start (hopefully scoring the first one or two goals) and to give us a chance to gauge the opponent. An effective coach can wisely balance development and immediate success.

It may not be politically correct, but everyone likes to win.

That includes me, the coach. It very definitely includes the kids. And it includes every single parent on the sidelines of a game. When kids see their new skills and principles working, they're motivated to work even harder and to stick with soccer. To me, that's the right system for the developmental place your kids are now.

It is important that this system be compatible with what they will do later on, and that's not hard to do, either. Just as the advice in this book builds upon all the principles I set out in *Coaching Little Kid Soccer,* the layers of the basic game approach I'll show you here will lay the groundwork for even more complex elements of the game to be added down the road in a way that feels natural to players.

So, even if you yourself have never played, coached, or watched big-time soccer – or even any soccer – I will show you a simple, effective approach to the elementary game that will allow your team of random players with varying levels of skill and experience to play well individually and as a team and to improve noticeably during the season. And I will show you how to coach them so you'll have a good chance at beating the team coached by a former college player or the local high school coach in charge of his daughter's under-8 team. You'll probably find beating those coaches as fun as I do.

This is an approach that works both for recreational soccer, where you will have many players who are new to the sport or who are mainly there for fun and exercise, and also for more serious league soccer like Quinn plays, where virtually every player comes onto the team with some skills and experience and hopes to play at a more competitive level in the future.

In this book, I'm giving you the system I've developed, which was shaped by lots of tips and observations shared by other coaches – and especially by working with Quinn and his teammates.

I believe it will get you on your way to a great season. If you've never coached before and your first practice is in a few days, you may want to read the Appendix: Team Management first to get everyone organized.

2

The essence of elementary soccer

As I encouraged in *Coaching Little Kid Soccer*, try to put yourself in the mindset of each child at each practice and game. Remember being this age, and think of what your own child this age has taught you so far. Look for clues about how the kids are experiencing what you're showing them, especially whether they understand or whether they may have mistaken assumptions.

Portrait of the age

Unlike the preschoolers they recently were, these are elementary kids who are gaining increasing responsibility and independence. At school, they're given roles to play like line leader or library aide and are able to perform them. They should have responsibilities and chores around the house. If that's not true at your house, teach your son or daughter how to load and unload the dishwasher – it'll change your life!

In general, I find that kids this age are much more capable and can be more responsible than the adults in their lives give them credit for. The fact that they will make flatulence noises in their armpits during an idle moment does not contradict this truth! That's an amusing new skill they picked up today in their spare time and are proudly practicing and showing off.

My approach is to give each kid as much responsibility as he or she can handle, dialing that back if it's a little too much, rather than just assuming where the edges of their capabilities are or keeping things easy for them, something many parents seem to want. Good coaching, like good parenting, is a balance: stretching a child to expand his limits while never setting her up to fail.

Many kids will be in the swing of participating in league sports by now, with three, five, or even eight seasons of soccer and/or other sports under their belts. Others will be new or inexperienced at it, and you'll have to quickly bring them up to speed, making a point to tutor them along the way so they don't get utterly discouraged by their more skilled and experienced teammates. You also have to explain to the new kid that the other players are better because they've been working at it and practicing longer, and that if the new kid does the same, he will get better, too.

And don't forget that you're doing something fundamentally important for these elementary-schoolers. You're giving kids with a ton of energy who have been sitting still all day in a classroom the chance to run and compete and be noisy and blow off steam, to get their heart rates up and sweat.

At the same time, unlike little kid soccer, you can and should expect more order and patience from elementary players. For preschool soccer, I never chose practice activities where kids had to wait their turn in line, because it was impossible for such young children. I kept all the kids moving all the time, never making them wait.

For elementary soccer, I still try to keep everyone moving four-fifths of the time, but it's now reasonable to expect players to stand and watch and wait their turn as other players do a short one-on-one drill. But at this age, still only for a short portion of practice.

The basics of elementary soccer

Like little kid soccer, elementary soccer is often co-ed and should be played "short-sided," or with fewer than an adult team's 11 players on the field at one time. Our under-8 league has five players per team on the field at a time, including the goalie (abbreviated 5 v. 5.) Our team plays in an inter-league recreational tournament where the rule is 6 v. 6.

The reason for fewer than 11 players on the field is that it gives each player more responsibility and a lot more time and space during the game to play rather than waiting around all the time to get involved in a play. It also allows for there to be specialized positions: defenders, midfielders and forwards, but with fewer of each, so position play is simpler and there is more real estate for each one to be in charge of.

The exact details of game play will vary from place to place, which won't matter too much (having five on a side rather than six makes very little difference, for instance). Some new features of the game not usually present in soccer at younger ages include:

- During games, the coaches are usually restricted to the sideline (maybe even a small section of the sideline designated as a coaching box) rather than being allowed on the field with their teams. The league usually provides referees, so that coaches no longer officiate the game.
- As such, leagues often formally keep score of these games and declare a winner rather than playing just for fun.
- Each team plays one goalie who wears a different jersey and is allowed to touch the ball with his hands inside the goalie box, while little kid soccer usually uses tiny goals with no goalkeepers.
- When one team makes the ball go out of play across one of the sidelines, a player from the other team returns it to play with a throw-in. (See "Throw-ins" in Chapter 8.)
- When the defending team makes the ball go out of

bounds across its own endline (beside its goal), the other team returns the ball to play with a corner kick. (See "Corner Kicks" in Chapter 8.)
- When the offensive team makes the ball go across the endline next to the goal they're trying to attack, the defense returns the ball to play with a goal kick. (See "Goal Kicks" in Chapter 8.)

There are several big, important strategies I teach at this level. In Chapter 6, I'll show them to you in the order that your players need to understand them, which is therefore the order that you need to teach them.

You can seriously teach your team the first strategy, which is understanding goal rectangles, in practice the first week and show them nothing else before your first game on Saturday, and they will be just fine. If they show you they understand it and can put it into action, go ahead and add the next idea in practice next week while still reinforcing the first. If they need serious work, just continue to focus on the first strategy.

Your coaching mindset

You are in the right mindset to coach your son's or daughter's elementary soccer team when you:
- Understand where your child and her peers are developmentally and build your coaching plan around that understanding
- Want them to have fun, get exercise, and learn about teamwork and overcoming adversity as much as you want them to succeed at soccer
- Keep in mind that practices and games are about the players and what they need to develop as players and people, not about you or about the parents
- Are able to be firmly in charge while laughing, playing, being patient, and having fun with them.

3

Bryan's elementary principles

Look what's new: Soccer is a team game

Early elementary-grade players are finally able to play soccer as a team game. And that is SO much fun. In fact, I'd say that's the most important thing they're learning right now in soccer.

I said in *Coaching Little Kid Soccer* that I didn't teach preschoolers to pass because preschoolers are self-centered and lack the coordination to pass, and I'd never seen one successfully able to do it in a game. But elementary kids *are* now mature enough to pass and to decide when they should and shouldn't do so. They can cooperate rather than playing completely self-centered like preschoolers do. When they do, amazing things will happen.

To cooperate as a team, they must learn to play the different specialized field positions on the team, including what to do and avoid doing in each. This is not a chore: Believe me, they find this fascinating to learn and do. And it is so much fun to teach and watch.

All the kids learn all the jobs

You and I will teach every kid on our team to do every single one of these "jobs," as I call them, (since kids this age don't immediately know the term, "positions.") We will teach them – and let them do in real games – all of the jobs, because they are all still developing as players, and because they all deserve the years of time they need to discover which position is the most fun and natural for them. They can specialize later if they choose to continue with soccer at an advanced level. Both now and in the future, they can play their own position better when they have had experience at the other jobs.

This playing all positions concept is personal to me. As a recreational player Quinn's age, I was a tall, uncoordinated kid growing so fast that I didn't know where the ends of my arms and legs arms were. I was pigeonholed as a defender and never even got to try playing midfield or offense. Or goalie. I spent my playing time standing on the edge of the goalie box waiting for the play to come to my end of the field, and when it did, I would stop the dribbler and boot the ball back into the other half of the field and watch longingly as the forwards and midfielders attacked the goal.

I always dreamed of scoring a goal during a game. But I never even got to take a shot.

I was never coached to dribble the ball on defense, so I never picked up that skill, either. But every one of my players in under-8 gets the opportunity to score a goal in almost every single game, and virtually all of them are able to put one into the net for the team at some point in our season.

(The worst part is, I discovered at age 28 that I didn't even get coached about how to play defense correctly. I joined an adult recreational team and got straightened out on it!)

Reward correct decisions regardless of the result

I remember vividly being this age and knowing exactly what I wanted my lanky body to do. I wanted to kick the ball down the sideline to my midfielder. I kicked at it, but hit it at the wrong angle, and it went out of bounds. My coach would yell, "Why'd you kick it out of bounds?" Well, I didn't mean to! I'd made the right decision. I just hadn't succeeded in carrying it out.

At this age, the first thing the players need to master is knowing the right thing to do and then trying to do it. I call that making good decisions. No matter how a play turns out, I praise players for making solid decisions.

Often, because kids are developing their skills, it's not obvious what they meant to do based on what you see happening in the game. So I am constantly asking them: "Cameron, was that a pass or a shot?" You should get into this habit, too. I find kids to be very forthcoming about what they were trying to do.

If a shot was the right decision, I praise Cameron for deciding to shoot, even if he misses the shot. If he should have passed, I take a few seconds and explain why and get a nod in return. If he doesn't respond, I say, "Do you understand?" until I get an acknowledgement.

Often, one player will do exactly what she needs to do in a situation, and a teammate will neglect to do his part, with a bad result such as our team losing possession of the ball. Though the ultimate result was bad, I make a point to notice and praise the first player's correct decision. Of course, you should also constructively explain to the second player how and why she made the wrong one.

What you're really teaching

It's so easy to get fixated on those soccer skills. And we'll work on those in just a little bit.

But let's remember first that the more important things you are teaching kids are concepts that are key to their emotional and psychological development:

Exercise is fun and feels great: You have the chance to show members of a generation of kids who will spend unprecedented amounts of time indoors in front of gadget screens that it is delightful and healthy to be outdoors moving your body.

Working hard is how you get better: The first practice of each season, I have my players run four sprints the length of the field with just a few seconds break between them. Most of the kids get seriously winded. I explain to them that by the end of the season, they'll be ready for a fifth or a sixth or seventh sprint because they will work this season to get their bodies used to running. At the last practice, I have them do it and I point out that their work is the reason they increased their ability.

You can compete hard in an appropriate way: As I was coaching my very first team of preschoolers, I suddenly realized that the kids were not playing very well because they had been taught by their families that you always have to share and take turns. Elementary kids, it seems, know all about competition, but they need you to teach them to compete graciously with sportsmanship and empathy.

One tradition I instill in my players is to drop to one knee on the field whenever the game stops because someone is injured. We take a knee and turn toward the player and wait for him to get up and resume play or to be taken off the field for care. And when the player is up, we applaud.

In rare instances where an opposing player is down and apparently hurt and the referee doesn't see, I tell my players to intentionally kick the ball out over the sideline to stop play. The longstanding soccer tradition is that once the player is tended to, the other team should throw the ball in and then deliberately play it gently to your team's goalkeeper, to restore possession to your team in a return gesture of sportsmanship. Some refs and coaches in your league won't know this tradition, so you have to be willing to give up a turnover to ensure the player gets helped, and you should be willing to do that. It is a great example to set for your players.

If your team is much better than the opponent, you as the coach should avoid running up the score. I try to keep our goal total to 10 or fewer unless the other team has a similar number. I let my kids play full speed until we have about a five-goal lead. Then, I impose rules on our play that make it more difficult for us to score while also making us practice skills we need to get better. I might insist on a pass before each shot. I might move my good scorer to defense and put a player new to offense in as a forward. I might tell every child who has already scored they may only shoot with their non-dominant foot.

So, against strong competition, we play our hardest. We directly challenge opposing players. We seek to win. But we don't grab, push, or talk trash. We don't brag when we're winning nor taunt opposing players. We're not obnoxious brats when we lose fair and square. We shake hands and move on.

You can learn to manage your feelings: There are two aspects to how we handle any situation, the way we initially, impulsively feel about it, and the ways we choose to respond to that emotion. Most grownups actually could stand to get better at this, but elementary kids definitely need work. The other guy took the ball away from you when you were about to score! You're mad about it! You can flop down and have a tantrum. You can trip him and get whistled for a foul. Or you can run after him and try to get the ball back fair and square.

You have to teach kids this two-stage process: the feeling that just comes and the choice they have to make about how to respond to that feeling. Never say, "Don't be angry" or "Don't cry." Validate their feeling: "You're frustrated." "That really hurt." "You're disappointed because you hoped you were about to score a goal, and it didn't work out."

Don't assume a child can't control his resulting behavior, either. Show him the choice he made. "You chose to hit him." "You responded by sitting down and giving up." Ask what different choice he could have made. If he really doesn't see any, list some possible ones you saw available. Praise mature decisions: "You took a tumble and looked upset, but you jumped back up and got back into the play – way to go." If a kid fails to manage his feelings right away, pull him out for a break to give him time to regain control and motivate him to do so.

We persevere through adversity: Especially if you're coaching middle-class kids, many of them have not experienced – or learned to overcome – much hardship. But a little bit of manageable hardship develops the crucial life skill of positive perseverance. I find myself constantly telling my kids things like, "Yes, getting kicked in the ankle really hurts. But there is no blood and you can wiggle it. You can keep going."

Kids who are comfortable most of the time are amazed and so satisfied when they find they can overcome a little setback or do a little bit more than they thought they could, or that they don't have to melt into a puddle over every discomfort and minor disappointment. If you treat it like the end of the world, they will treat it as a major setback. If you show you expect them to move past it, they will rise to your challenge.

Obviously, you have to use sound judgment. If a kid is having a heat stroke, or is bleeding, or severely upset, don't tell him to power through. It's that same principle of stretching kids just a little bit but never pushing them too hard.

You have to learn to cooperate, even with people who irritate you: Kids need to learn how to adapt to randomly assigned teammates they wouldn't have chosen, to respect and utilize each person's skills, and to work with them to accomplish a common objective. They need to see that the coach is their leader, that she may have a different style than other leaders that they've worked under, and that they need to adapt to that style. They need to follow their leader's instructions and ask questions when they are not sure.

Don't you wish everyone at your grownup job knew how to do all of these things better?

4

The disciplines of practice mirror the game

My training sessions are set up to teach players about the key aspects of the game and to get them to handle those aspects in a disciplined way. You can find a million random soccer drills on the Internet. Lots of them are fun, and many teach certain skills. Yet some bear very little resemblance to actual soccer game play. The less they are like actual play, the less I like them.

I set up my practice sessions both to consciously and subconsciously instill the rhythm and disciplines of the game in my players. Here are some key aspects of the game I emphasize, and how I do it:

There are rules, and an adult is in charge

Just as the referee is in control of Saturday's game, you, the coach, are overseeing what the players do on the practice field, and you are the authority over what happens in practice – and what stops happening.

As kids arrive to first practice, meet each one, ask his or her name, and tell the player what you would like to be called. I might say, "Hello, I'm Coach Bryan. What's your name?" I have a friendly conversation and give the child a smile and a fist bump, but I also want them to leave this conversation with the clear sense that I'm in charge and will tell them what they need to do and not do. When you present yourself this way, parents tend to reinforce your authority: "Jaden, listen to your coach. Follow his instructions." Speaking of that, I seek to give a few instructions right as I meet each kid: "Get your shoes tied, please, and join us over here." Or, "Wearing that ninja necklace could be dangerous, so give it your dad and come back here as soon as you've done it."

This also means that as practice begins, you're consciously setting a precedent that you will not tolerate kids disregarding your instructions. I have seen coaches try to ignore a child's misbehavior and totally lose control over practice. The problem is that the renegade child quickly becomes a distraction to others, and if teammates see the rebel getting away with it, they get the message they can do anything they want.

You don't have to be unfriendly or overly stern. You just have to exert your authority. First, you name wrong behavior and give a clear instruction for it to stop (including what the child *should* do instead.)

If, after a warning, a child still doesn't comply with your instructions, get down onto one knee, put your hand firmly on his shoulder and look him in the eye: "Javier, you are yanking on Sandy's shirt when you need to be listening to me – even after I reminded you a few minutes ago. When you're at practice, you must follow my directions. Leave your ball here, and go sit with your mother and think about that." After a few minutes, go over to Javier and ask him (not his mom), "Javier, are you ready to follow my instructions now?" If he answers yes, say, "Okay, come back to the group." If he doesn't answer or the answer is no, walk away and leave the child with his parent. Nine out of 10 kids are back on the field and cooperating within a few minutes, usually after the parent reinforces your authority. If a child won't cooperate, he can't participate until he changes that.

You also reinforce your authority in the positive aspects of your relationship with each player. By using humor, showing children empathy, taking a kid aside for individualized tutoring, tending to them when they're hurt, and listening closely to what they say to you and ask of you, you build a mutual trust. I find this motivates them toward their best behavior and soccer.

No hands – feet!

In many cases, kids will arrive dribbling their ball. But often a kid is carrying it. Give this instruction: "Okay, Jackson, at soccer practice, we learn to use our bodies and feet to move our ball, never our hands, unless you are playing goalie. So I want you to put your ball on the ground right now and use your feet. All the players! All the players! No hands during practice unless you're the goalie or you're taking a throw-in. Only bodies and feet." Stand there until the child puts the ball down.

Enforce this rule all season any time the child is in your sight: when they are making their way to the practice or game field, heading back toward the car after practice (not in traffic!), or messing around before a game, if kids aren't playing goalie, they should be dribbling their ball, not throwing, catching or carrying it. You've just built in 15-30 extra minutes of ball-handling practice per week for each of your players.

And by establishing this discipline, you make manipulating the ball without the use of hands more natural and instinctive. That greatly reduces the chance that a child will reach out and use his hands on the ball during a game when it's not doing what they want.

We understand and respond to whistle signals

Long whistle means, "Let's begin." No later than five minutes after the scheduled start of practice, blow a long blast on your whistle and gather the team. "All the players! All the players! Dribble your ball here to me. Make a bunch of grapes with the balls right here next to Quinn's." The bunch of grapes is a great way to move from every child having his or her own ball to an activity where you want only one or none. It's also a great way to reduce distractions when you're speaking to the kids.

A referee will use a long whistle blast to start the game, and that's why you use one to start practice.

Double whistle means take a break and look for instructions. A referee blows a double whistle blast to signal the end of a game quarter or half, pausing play. You'll use the same signal in practice to let the kids know they are entering a transition time and need to look to the adult in charge for instructions. Blow a double whistle to change to a new practice activity or to declare a water break.

Triple whistle means the session is finished: When practice is done, give a tweet-tweet-*tweet!* Just like the ref does when time has expired. (Note: Some referees use double and triple whistle blasts interchangeably.)

A sharp whistle blast means freeze! As soon as I start the very first practice, I explain to the players, "All the players! All the players! Any time you are at soccer and you hear this sound (I demonstrate a short, sharp whistle blast), you freeze right where you are. If you're dribbling a ball, put your foot on top of it and freeze." I blow the whistle. "Freeze like a statue!" They do it. Then we go right into a practice game (I hate the word drill) that I call Stop/Go.

In this game, all the players dribble their balls at the same time in any meandering pattern they choose, and when I blow the whistle, they freeze and stop the ball by putting their foot on top of it. When they do, I point at each child still moving until he finally freezes. I praise the ones who do it quickest, and playfully point out who took a long time, "Oh, Marcel, got to be quicker at freezing than that." I also point out to the players that they must keep their ball close to their feet to have such tight control that they can stop the ball in an instant, a great ball handling lesson.

Now that you've established this discipline, any time things get unsettled, tweet your whistle and point at kids slow to freeze. It works really well. And the bonus is that in games, when the ref blows the whistle, your kids will instantly stop instead of dribbling along oblivious like kids from other teams.

We run as a team

As you will see later, we'll teach our offense to run up and down the field in a coordinated way (with players advancing toward the goal the way the edge of a wave advances up the beach). Watch Premier League soccer or the big-time pro soccer of your choice, and you will see the pros doing this: The fullbacks will be in a roughly straight line across the field. The forwards will advance on the opposing goal as a unit spread across the width of the field.

I like to begin practice with sprints the length of the field – which is, again, what players will need to do time after time in the game. The kids all line up along one endline, all on the same side of the goal, like racers on the starting line. Only this isn't a race! It's a secret team-building exercise, and best of all, it mimics the flow of the game, where you run up and down the field.

I say, "Everybody jump up and down on this line. When I say go, you run to the other end of the field and jump up and down on THAT white line. When they're all pogo-ing, I say, "Ready, set – go!" and they all sprint to the opposite endline. You may choose to run the sprints with your team, but be warned, second graders and above will often be faster than you and have better stamina!

Here is the key to this exercise: the first players to reach the end pogo on the line until ALL the other kids get there and join them. Then I pick a child and say, "Madeline, say, 'Ready, set – go!' " And with delight, she'll yell it, and we'll all run back to the other endline, as I encourage them to, "Goooo!" Give a few other kids a turn to be the leader and make at least three trips up and down the field. You can mix it up by sometimes having everyone stop at the midline and then either continue to the opposite endline after everyone gets there or reverse back to the endline where you just were.

Another variation is to pick two of the players to be "rabbits" and have them begin first while the others try to catch them. This simulates chasing down an opposing player on a fast break to our goal.

If we fall down, we jump up immediately

Kids will fall down a lot. When one does, immediately urge her, "Jump back up!" It is dangerous in a game for a child to stay on the ground. He can get stepped on, and other kids can fall on top of him.

Some kids intentionally dive and roll around on the ground, and you shouldn't tolerate this behavior. When you do get kids trained to hop up instantly – and then one doesn't – you blow the whistle and make everyone freeze while you run over to him, because then you know it's probably a real injury.

5

No more bunch ball

Elementary-school soccer players should no longer follow the ball around in a clump. That's chaos, and it's hard for kids to make sense of chaos. Just like at your job, teamwork happens only when everyone has a role, understands how to play that role, has the skills needed to play that role, and understands the roles of others – and trusts that they'll do their jobs, too.

As I said earlier, you will teach every child how to play all the positions and give him or her game experience in each one during the season. You may be as surprised as I was at first that kids this age – even the most shrimpy straggler – really are able to learn to do all the positions reasonably well.

They definitely have their preferences, sometimes instilled by their parents and sometimes one they just think seems cool (often totally unrelated to which one they are actually best at!). One kid told me his favorite position was "player." He meant "not being goalie." Some kids need a little or a lot more practice or coaching for certain jobs, but they can all learn all the jobs. So they should.

When my team is up big over a less skilled or practiced team – say 6-0 – to avoid running up the score more, I often put my players into our weakest configuration. That is, I put each of my players in the job where he or she has the most trouble or the most to learn. This gives players the chance to try what we've been learning in practice and for me to show them that the principles work and why (against not the strongest opponent, remember), and to reinforce what they are learning using real game situations.

Set up like this, our team often continues to score goals, probably at a slower pace than before, and we usually continue to prevent the other team from scoring any or many on us, though it usually takes a bit more effort. In this way, we're able to get something beneficial out of the game, including a challenge for our players, and to offer the same to our opponents.

We play positions

But why does our weakest lineup still outmatch other teams? Simply because we are spreading out and trying to play positions during the whole game, and they probably aren't.

A lot of teams we face line their kids up in positions for kickoff but don't really stick to them after that, devolving to preschool herd-ball. And let me tell you, really playing positions will beat a team that doesn't know how nearly every single time, regardless of the skills of individual players. Three kids on the same team standing in a clump on the field essentially reduces them to the effectiveness of a single player. If they start competing with each other to possess the ball – and they will – it's like they're giving players to our team.

This effect is so strong that a team of five players playing positions will beat a team of six or seven playing swarm ball nearly every single time.

Lines: So what are the positions? Goalie is a special case I'll discuss later. For now, let's talk about the regular field players. For my under-6 team, I assigned just two lines, or categories, of player: offense and defense. The two jobs are clearly distinguished: Rebecca, Jimmy and Jamal range up the field and try to score goals. Caitlin stays back near our goal and stops people from advancing on our goal and scoring.

But for under-8, even with 5 v. 5 play, I encourage you to use a goalkeeper plus all of the three lines of position found at the most advanced levels of soccer: forwards or offensive players, midfielders or halfbacks, and defenders or fullbacks. Adding midfielders at the U8 level is something other coaches had to urge me to try after I was initially reluctant. I decided they were right after I did try.

Of course, a midfielder shares a little of both jobs: When we're on the attack, the midfielder goes along and may take shots on goal, just like a forward does. The midfielders play somewhat behind the offense most of the time, recovering a ball that the other team kicks away from our offense and so forth. And when the other team gets possession of the ball, the midfielders are the first to sprint back toward our goal to help defend it.

Each individual job comes with two basic types of guideline: the main tasks outlined just now, and also some home real estate where the player should spend most of his time and return after leaving it only for special opportunities and emergencies.

Lanes: Imagine the soccer field split in half longways into right and left halves (right and left from our team's perspective as we face the goal we're attacking). A player assigned to right offense or right defender should start out in the right half of the field and range only as far as the midline, or slightly over it, except in cases of extreme opportunity or emergency. A player on the left stays mostly to the left of the line. A player assigned to a center role, such as center offense, should start on that midline and range right and left from there, but normally not all the way to the sideline.

I call these overlapping right, middle and left strips of the field "lanes," and I teach players, "stay in your lane." When I first introduce the concept, I use orange cones to mark the long midline on the practice field as a visual reminder. You could also choose to divide the field into thirds with cones, but I think this gives kids an over-precise idea of the lane boundaries.

It is very, very hard at first for kids to discipline themselves to stay in their lane. In fact, they forget; they stray; they get sucked into the action 30 yards from where they are supposed to be. I call them on it. I'll blow the whistle, freeze everyone on the field, and let them notice where they are versus where they need to be. I'll make them return to the right area during the pause before re-starting. At first, some get really frustrated with me: "But coach! The *ball* isn't in my lane. It's over there!"

I explain that even though the *ball* is elsewhere, it's *still* the player's job to stay in his lane. Staying in our lanes disciplines us to stand in empty space. When we claim empty space, good things will happen. Our teammate surrounded by half the other team in a bunch can kick the ball into our space, and we'll have a lot of room to control it and dribble it with no opponents anywhere near. If we're playing defense and stay in our lane, we don't let the attacking player beat two of us with a single move or leave his teammate open to receive a pass.

On offense, lanes are particularly important. Our right forward dribbles down the right side of the field. The center forward is so tempted to go over and join him. But the center forward's job is to stay in the middle lane. I will shout a running cadence of, "Middle, middle, middle, middle, middle!" to remind the center forward to stay middle, and to remind the right forward his job is to kick the ball into the middle.

I love the moment when a skeptical center forward follows my instruction to do that and then sees his teammate roll the ball across the mouth of the goal for the first time, no defenders within a mile, setting up the kid to score.

That's when a kid becomes a believer in playing positions.

Playing in lines AND lanes: Each set of players in the same role should move up and down the field roughly even with each other horizontally – in a horizontal line. So if I have three forwards, they should move up the field like cars door to door in three parallel freeway lanes. They move as a line.

For 5 players versus 5 players, or 5 v. 5, matches, I have used all of these setups at various times (in order from most aggressive/risky to most defensive/unlikely to score us a lot of points):

- 1 goalie, 1 defender, 1 midfielder, 2 forwards
- 1 goalie, 1 defender, 2 midfielders, 1 forward
- 1 goalie, 2 defenders, 1 midfielder, 1 forward

If it's 6 v. 6, I might play:

- 1 goalie, 1 defender, 1 midfielder, 3 forwards
- 1 goalie, 1 defender, 2 midfielders, 2 forwards
- 1 goalie, 1 defender, 3 midfielders, 1 forward
- 1 goalie, 2 defenders, 2 midfielder, 1 forward

You'll notice that because we play so short-sided, you will often play a lineup where there's only one player in a line. When there is just one player in a line, that player can play the width of the field, but should generally play the home real estate of a player assigned to the center lane.

Getting out of "shape," and back into it: As the game proceeds, for various reasons (compelling opportunity, emergency, or simply from losing focus and drifting), players will stray from their home real estate. The key is simply that once the reason for leaving their space is no longer true, or once they realize they've drifted, they must make a point of getting back to their area. You'll spend a lot of your coaching time reminding them!

The soccer term for good spacing of players on the field is "shape." This isn't a term I use with kids at this age, since it's a little bit abstract. Instead, I stress for each child to know where on the field she needs to be given where the ball is and what's happening in the game.

A more subtle aspect of shape is changing your position on the field so that you open passing opportunities for your teammates. But at first, we'll settle for being in your line and lane and not having every player drawn to the ball as if it were a black hole. If your shape gets bent, straighten it out. And you do that player by player. Shout a player's name and ask him to reassess where he is: "Connor, are you where you're supposed to be?" Often, you'll find that the other players hear you and reconsider where they should be, as well.

Next, I'll give you my master strategies. And after that, I'll offer special guidance you can share with each line of players on how best to do their job.

6

The master strategies

There are strategies unique to each position you assign a kid to play on the field, which I'll cover later. But the first strategies you should teach – and the ones that will have the biggest effect – are the ones that apply to the whole team. These are the things I advise you to teach first, and in this order.

Seriously, if you gave me a whole team of players I had never coached before with a single 20-minute practice before our first game, I would teach them Master Strategy No. 1 below, goal rectangles, and feel pretty good about how we were about to do in a game against their age mates.

Master Strategy: Play the defensive and offensive goal rectangles

This most fundamental strategic idea is one I also taught to preschoolers: When we are defending our goal, we of course don't want the other team to kick the ball into our net, scoring on us. What's not obvious to kids, though, is that the most effective way to do that is to keep the ball from ever rolling into what I call "our rectangle," the area in front of the mouth of our goal.

I'm *not* talking about the rectangular penalty area or the goal-kick box that are marked on the field. I'm talking about an imaginary rectangle the same width as the goal uprights extending about 15-20 yards toward middle of the field. If you think about the goal as the household garage in which you'd park a car, this rectangle is the driveway to it. I tell the kids, "Keep it out of our rectangle." To keep the ball out of our net, we *first* keep it out of the real estate from which other players are going to be able to take solid shots. If the car never touches the driveway, it can't get into the garage.

There are three important ways to achieve this:
- Have players challenge any player who tries to dribble into our rectangle, so we can steal the ball or make him change direction or kick it away.
- Dribble or kick a loose ball rolling toward or into our rectangle back out of the rectangle.
- Never dribble or kick the ball into our rectangle ourselves! (Kids don't know not to do this unless you stress it with them. Also, note that at higher levels of soccer, players do purposely play the ball to their goalkeeper or to a fullback, but I don't suggest it until age 10 or higher. That's an exception to the rule, so teach them the rule first.)

The goal rectangles principle is exactly reversed on the other end of the field, around the goal we are attacking. Kids understand the idea of wanting to kick the ball into the net. But when a kid dribbles down the sideline into the corner on the offensive end, what does he do then? He's at such a sharp angle to the goal that he has no realistic shot. He may not be able to spot a teammate.

So our first job on offense is just to get the ball *into* the rectangle leading to the other team's goal. We could try to dribble it in there or kick it there. From the rectangle, our player has great shooting angles. If we kick the ball into or across the other team's rectangle, a teammate should be hanging around there, able to finish the job of parking the ball in the back of the net.

Get this: I will praise an offensive player for kicking the ball from the corner across the mouth of the other team's goal even if there's not a teammate within 50 yards of it. That player did her job. Rather than getting stuck down in the corner like 90 percent of kids her age, she crossed the ball into the goal rectangle. It's another player's job to be waiting there.

When I first teach this idea, all I want is for the ball to be dribbled and kicked into the rectangle in front of the goal we are attacking, over and over. When our other players realize this will be a regular occurrence, they'll get onto the other end of those balls and shoot them. (Also, because other teams may be playing herd ball, often their defenders are all where the ball starts, with none waiting in the middle, anyway.)

When your team gets really good at this concept, you'll often have one of your players waiting in the center in front of the goal, and another to the far side of him in case the first player can't control the ball. Which is perfect.

Master Strategy: Maintain possession of the ball

We want our team to be in charge of the ball as much of the time as possible. Other youth sports like basketball tend to emphasize maintaining possession much more than most coaches do in soccer. You don't hear much talk of "turnovers" when soccer is discussed. Indeed, in many soccer games, possession changes very frequently and that's considered normal.

Within the space of 30 seconds, possession can go back and forth five times. That *can* happen. But we will teach our team to make individual decisions so that our team gains and keeps possession for long stretches. (But wait: Didn't I just tell you to have kids cross the ball on offense heedless of whether a teammate is there to collect it? Yes. But if we turn over the ball on the other team's end of the field while trying to cross and score, it's usually not a big disaster for us like turning it over in front of the mouth of our goal is. The potential advantage outweighs the disadvantage.)

Clearly, when the other team doesn't have control of the ball, they cannot score on us (we can mess up and kick or fumble the ball into our own goal, it's true, but this is another reason we don't kick or dribble into our own rectangle). Of course, when we do have control of the ball, we do have the chance to score on them.

These ideas are not obvious to your players before you teach them. Kids have the instinct just to kick the ball upfield when it comes to them, often not with any clear purpose. You will give them a purpose so they can make a more productive decision, and you will expect them to make one.

First, we gain possession. The first thing we need is for one of our players to have control of the ball.

Our team gets control of the ball by:
- Starting with it at kickoff.
- Being awarded a throw-in, goal kick, or corner kick after the other team causes the ball to go out of bounds.
- Winning races to loose balls that are rolling or bouncing around the field under no one's control, and bringing them under our control.
- Challenging an opposing player who has control of the ball and taking control of the ball away from him or her.
- Intercepting the other team's attempted pass or shot.

So I teach players, "First, one of us gets control." For the first two situations in my list above, this happens automatically. For the last three, though, how do we make it happen?

Bringing the ball under control: When I was growing up and playing youth soccer, I was taught to "trap the ball." We spent a lot of time in practice learning how to use our feet and bodies to bring a moving ball to a dead stop. Sometimes this is useful in a game. But much more often, a player just needs the ball to be in a space where she knows she can usefully act on it again without another player interfering. This means that when gaining control of a loose ball or receiving a pass from a teammate, it's usually either fine or advantageous for the ball to continue moving.

Therefore, controlling the ball just means to make it do something productive with my very first touch. I tap it on ahead to my teammate. Or I make it bounce near my feet where I can have another useful touch after my first one.

So when a goalie punt is flying toward me, I don't have to be so ambitious as to bring that ball to a dead stop at my feet. I just have to use my body on it to direct the ball into some empty space where I can then get to it first and make another move on it. If it bounces off my chest and rolls into open ground in the direction of the other team's goal where I can catch up to it easily, that's great. That's having control. If a teammate kicks the ball 10 feet in front of me, and I run toward it and get to it first, that's control. Maybe I stick out my foot to deflect that ball into some free space where I can pick up my dribble: control.

It's really that simple: I have control when I know that I or a teammate I have in mind will be the next player to act on the ball.

Master Strategy: Our players make quick, smart decisions with the ball

During the process of getting control, a player necessarily stares at the ball. Yet once a player knows she has control, I want her to change her focus and make a decision. This requires looking up and making a visual scan to get information about what's happening elsewhere on the field with opponents and teammates. It's absolutely not natural for most kids to shift their focus like this, so you have to teach them to make doing so a habit.

I train my player to *"Look up!"* To actually shift focus *away* from the ball that has just been her center of focus, now that she knows it's hers, and to assess the three – yes, exactly three – best choices available to her: Shoot? Dribble? Or pass?

1. **Shoot?** Now I have control of the ball. I look up. Am I near the goal we're attacking? Do I see a clear path for the ball to travel to go into the goal? Am I capable of kicking the ball along that path? Is there a good chance defenders or the goalie won't be able to block my shot? If the answer to all of those questions is yes, I should shoot. If the answer to any is no, the answer to whether I should shoot is also no.

2. **Dribble?** Is there clear space near me into which I can advance the ball toward the goal we're attacking or into a more advantageous position by dribbling? (*Not* into our own goal rectangle, and not close to a player I think can take the ball from me. As I said, at this age, I do not teach the players to dribble or pass backward toward our own goal, as it can too easily help the other team score on us if something goes awry.) If the answer to the question is yes, then the answer to whether I should dribble is probably yes.

3. **Or Pass?** Is a teammate closer to the goal we're attacking than I am? Is one or more opposing players very close to me or bearing down on me to steal the ball? Is a teammate of mine in open space without defenders around? When the answer to these questions is yes, I should pass.

What's a pass, really? In my youth soccer days, we were taught that a pass was kicking the ball exactly to your teammate's foot, where he could trap it, or bring it to a dead stop. That's really precise and really hard for kids this age (or anyone) to do. Fortunately, that's not really what a pass is at even the most elite levels of soccer. A running player doesn't usually want the ball to come exactly to him or to stop dead.

A pass is kicking the ball where my teammate can get it first. If he's standing still, that can mean right to his foot. But usually – and this is a lot easier to accomplish – it should mean kicking the ball into empty space in front of or beside my teammate where he or she can definitely get there first and gain control of it.

Kids have to be taught that when a teammate is running, they can't kick the ball to where their teammate is. They have to anticipate and kick it where the teammate's about to be, to the place they're running toward. And this space needs to be empty of opposing players. When kids learn this, they're amazed. Knowing the pass can be approximate and into empty space gives kids much more confidence to try it and get better at it during games. They just have to put the ball where their teammate can get to it first.

Of course, the receiving players need you to teach them that when their teammate kicks a ball into empty space in front of them, their job is to run to the ball first and control it. It is really beautiful to watch kids begin to grasp and use these concepts, which are not obvious to them at all, as intuitive as they seem to us as adults. It's also very helpful if the passer shouts the name of the intended recipient to prompt that player to pay attention and to run to the ball.

Guess what? When the pass comes, and the receiving player runs to it and gains control, the whole process must begin again: 1. Control the ball. 2. Look up. 3. Shoot, dribble, or pass?

My players grow accustomed to me shouting, "Shoot? Dribble? Pass? … Shoot? Dribble? Pass?" when they gain possession of the ball in practice. And to me saying, "Good decision!" or asking them, "Was that the best decision?" or "Why did you make that decision?"

After being made initially, the decision must be revisited moment to moment. Okay, I dribbled 10 feet, and defender is headed for me: Can I shoot? Keep dribbling? Or should I pass?

If our players can correctly make – and execute – this decision tree each time, we'll seldom lose possession of the ball. As they get used to this way of playing, sophisticated things you could never have imagined will begin to happen. They will note where on the field they and their teammates and opponents are before receiving the ball. They will begin to be able to make their initial decision while gaining or even before they gain possession.

This is all learned, practiced behavior.

I said that shoot, dribble, and pass were the three best choices. There is one other possibility in case of emergencies: Kick the ball way upfield or out of bounds. Kids tend to overuse this option, though. I'm always helping them evaluate this decision when they make it and giving them feedback: "That was a real emergency; good decision to kick it out," or "You had time and space, Justin. Couldn't you have dribbled that ball or found a teammate to pass to instead?"

Master Strategy: Goals happen (for or against us) when the ball gets behind the defenders

Here's another precept that seems obvious to adults but that kids need you to explain: Most great goal scoring opportunities come when the ball advances past the defenders under the attacking team's control. That's when an attacker can shoot with only one person to beat, the goalie, who's a lot smaller than the goal itself. So:

While the other team has possession, we constantly place our bodies between the ball and our goal. If the other team's player has the ball, we want our players to begin, one at a time, putting themselves between the ball and our goal. Any time the other team's player has the ball with no one but the goalie between him and our goal, our closest player must rush to get between the ball handler and the goal.

Okay, so what if the other team's forward is dribbling toward our goal, and Meghan from our team is already getting into his path and closing the space? Here's a time when our other players are allowed to leave their home real estate or migrate to the very edge of it. But this is still *not* bunch ball. I don't want my second player Tomas to "help" Meghan by doing the same thing she's trying to do. I want Tomas to let Meghan do her job but to "back her up." If Tomas needs to leave his home area to do that because no one else is around, I won't fuss at Tomas for it. Once that job is done, though, Tomas needs to remember to return to his own turf.

Tomas should stand between Meghan and our goal, where he thinks the opponent will end up if he is able to beat Meghan with a dribble move.

What should Meghan do if she gets beaten like this? "Get back on defense." She should run to put her body back between the attacking player and our goal, likely backing up Tomas just like he just did for her.

We seek to put the ball behind the other team's defense where our player can get to it first. This business about goals happening when the ball is behind is as true on the half of the field away from our goal as in our own defensive half. We seek to exploit the behind-the-defense principle when we're on offense. It takes a lot of work to get players thinking about getting the ball behind the other team's defenders. There seems to be an instinct to dribble right through a defender, which rarely works out. We need some other tactics to accomplish this.

Here are the main ones:
- **Pass to a teammate.** I find that lateral passes – passing to a teammate who's beside me – come naturally first to young players. A lateral pass to a teammate who doesn't have a defender blocking his path can be a great way to set us up to get the ball behind the defense:
- **Kick it and follow it:** This is very nearly a pass to oneself. When facing down a defender who's about to come try to steal the ball from me, I can simply kick the ball to the side of him so that it rolls behind him into some empty space. When I do, I must sprint to the ball before he realizes what's happening. If I kick a ball like this, I must take off running and be the first to get there. If it works, I'll be behind the defense in possession of the ball. If our players can kick through-balls into big empty spaces behind the other team's defenders and can get to them first, we will score lots of goals.
- **A slick dribble move.** I won't get into the specific moves here, but if Charlotte can use her feet to suddenly

change the direction of the ball, or if she can feint right or left with her shoulders and get the defender to go that way while she dribbles the other, she can leave a defender behind off the dribble and get past him and behind the defense.
- **Through-balls:** It takes more imagination or training to play a "through-ball." All this means is that, if me and my teammate are facing a line of defenders, rather than passing sideways to where my buddy Miles is standing with a defender between Miles and the goal, I instead tap the ball downfield – past the other team's defenders – toward the goal, and into empty space Miles can easily run to. There, Miles can control it, and we'll have the ball behind the defense, looking to take a shot.

Master Strategy: Hassle their ball handler

Maybe this is really more of a master tactic that serves our earlier master strategies.

When our player encounters the other team's dribbler, we want our player to step into his path, as I've said. Then, we want our player to get closer to the dribbler, forcing the opponent to mess up, change direction or consider passing – or allow our player a chance to steal the ball. My sideline mantras for this are "stop that ball" or "go to him" or even "go take it."

How hassling their dribbler helps us: It slows the attack. It keeps the ball in front of our defenders, not behind them. It stops the ball from advancing into our goal rectangles. It helps our team re-gain possession.

Hassling how-to: When our closest player does get into that dribbler's path, we want him to move close to that player and put him to the test. It seems kids' natural instinct at this stage is actually to back up and allow space for an opposing player to advance the ball. A player may feel intimidated about challenging the opponent. Or this may be a side effect of the "take turns" training we've worked so hard on at school and the playground — it just doesn't seem very nice to take the ball the other player is using right now!

Teaching appropriate aggression: These hesitations are good in the rest of elementary life, but they're not good during a soccer game, so we have to teach a different behavior — appropriate aggression. (By the way, I hear a lot of other coaches hollering, "Be aggressive" to their players, especially after they see our players being aggressive, and it is clear their players have no real idea what that means! These are abstract terms you have to take care to define.)

This aggression is highly effective. Nine out of 10 opponents at this age are not particularly skilled dribblers. Often the sight of our aggressive team member closing the space is enough to make such a player lose composure as well as control of the ball. If that doesn't happen, our player can often go right up to the dribbler and tap the ball out of his control, winning possession. And, as I mentioned, if the dribbler beats one player, we soon send another after him.

Tailor to the opposing player: As we start a game against a new opponent, we should assume we can go take the ball from any of their players. Yet, the best opposing players at this level will be able to change direction with the ball or pass to get around our defender once she closes the space.

When we discover a skilled player like that, we'll handle him a little differently. We fall back to the objective of keeping our body between him and the goal rather than automatically closing down and trying to take the ball. This forces him to execute changes in direction, to stare down at the ball at his feet rather than looking for shooting or passing opportunities. It also blocks with our player's body many possible shots on goal or passes the player could try.

Sometimes, we cannot stop him; we can only hope to contain him: With a skilled player, we go for the ball only when the other player makes a mistake. That mistake is usually tapping the ball too hard while dribbling, putting the ball too far from the dribbler's own foot.

At higher levels of soccer this tactic must be used more and more. At this age, it's right to go try to take the ball away eight or nine times out of ten. In the British Premier League, by contrast, they play containment strategy nine-tenths of the time.

7

Position-specific strategies

Now, here are a few extra specifics about how you can coach your players to help accomplish these master strategies depending on what job (field position) you've assigned them.

Defenders (Fullbacks)

Of course, we want the fullbacks to keep the ball out of our goal rectangle. As I discussed before, their first job is to stop the ball from advancing by going to the dribbler and applying pressure when the ball enters their zone. For defenders, it's particularly important for them to know whether there's another defender backing them up.

For instance, if Claire's facing down an incoming dribbler and knows Javier is backing her up, she can be more aggressive with the dribbler, can "go to him" and try to win the ball. If she knows she's the last defender, she may simply try to stay between the aggressor and our goal and slow the advance of the ball until help can arrive.

Our defenders begin our next attack. One of my strong memories of my own youth soccer days is what the dad of my teammate Vikram would shout every time his son got possession of the ball as a fullback: "Boot the ball, Vikram!"

This was usually the wrong advice. A lot of players have the instinct simply to kick the ball as hard as they can whenever it comes to them, especially when playing defense and especially when they know their job is to keep it out of the goal rectangle. But the problem with this is that's at best a 50-50 chance of keeping possession.

Gaining possession on defense should actually give us an opportunity to begin an attack nearly every time. We seek to shoot, dribble, or pass, even – or perhaps especially – our defenders.

Of course, kicking the ball upfield, even way upfield, knowing you're putting it into a space where our midfielder or forward can get to it first constitutes a pass – and an excellent decision, very often the best one a defender can possibly make – because of course, when we can get the ball behind the other team's defenders where our player can get to it first, we should have a great chance to score. If you're not sure if that's what a player intended after a long kick, ask, "Who was that ball for?"

Players who've played defense for other coaches are often surprised to hear me say that they are not just allowed but encouraged to dribble as a defender as long as they have clear space. When a fullback controls a loose ball near the goalie box with no opponents around, that's in fact usually what I want: for him to dribble it upfield. And you know what? If no one challenges him, I'm fine with my defender dribbling all the way into the other team's rectangle and taking a shot. When this happens, it astonishes opposing teams, many of whom stand around waiting for him to pass because they have just never seen a defender do that. (It happens frequently in pro soccer.)

The player simply has to realize that his primary job is defense, so once he does pass – or get dispossessed – he has to sprint back to his home area and get back between the ball and our goal. Also, if our midfielders see a defensive player straying forward like this and aren't in a position to help with the attack, they need to play more defensively than normal to cover for our advancing player until the defender can get back into the usual shape.

Defensive emergencies: In an emergency, however, booting the ball may actually be the best choice. When we have the ball near our goal, and none of the preferred Shoot-Dribble-Pass options is available or if they all feel risky, that's probably an emergency: Arturo has the ball at his feet with four of their players closing in; the ball's rolling and about to go into our net or across the mouth of our goal; the ball is rolling toward the foot of their great shooter who's in a good position.

In cases like these, then it's legitimate to clear out the ball – simply to put it out of harm's way. But there's a right way to do that: Kick it away from our goal and toward a sideline, not toward the middle (an advantageous place for the other team to gain possession) or toward our net. Ideally, we'd kick it way up the sideline where one of our players had the chance to run and get it. Sometimes, we deliberately make it go out of bounds. In a pinch, we might kick it straight out of bounds or even out over our own endline, resulting in a corner kick for the other team. Never, never, never toward our net or across the mouth of our own goal.

A common defense coaching error is making defenders stand on the edge of the goalie box and just wait there when the play is way upfield. I instruct them to "sneak up" to or even across the midfield line, as long as they know they can get back quickly enough if needed. When defenders are forward like this, if a ball squirts out on the other team's end of the field, they can control it and pass to one of our offensive players, ensuring our team can continue the attack. They can also challenge a dribbler crossing midfield before he or she can pick up a lot of speed. This gives our midfielders time to "get back" and back up our stretched-forward defender.

A word about offsides: The offsides rule prohibits an attacking player from being behind the last non-goalie defender without having the ball. The rule becomes the key to much of the strategy of higher levels of soccer. Many leagues do not systematically enforce the offsides rule at this age (for one thing, it takes sideline assistant referees to enforce it well, and games at this age often have a single ref). But pushing the defense forward and limiting where the other team's players can stand will be a vital element of strategy at higher levels, and so it's a good habit for players to form now. It's also good to teach our players on offense not to be offsides now so that they don't have to re-imagine how to play offense later on when the rule will be enforced.

Midfielders (Halfbacks)

These players do a little of each job, offense and defense. When the game is in the offensive phase, they play offense, and when it is in a defensive phase, they help with defense. They must be able to do both jobs and to quickly make the transition between these two phases of the game, factoring into all their decisions the possible need to change roles on a moment's notice. These players also need a lot of physical endurance if you play them at midfield for long stretches, as they have to run a lot, often at a sprint. Of course, the alternative is to give players a short, intense shift and then rotate them to a new position or take them out for a rest.

When our team is attacking the opponents' goal, midfielders are part of the attack. If the forwards are bringing the ball up the field, midfielders might play behind the forwards to recover any loose ball, or even find some open space near the goal where a forward can pass to the midfielder for a shot.

If a midfielder has the ball, he or she might even pass the forwards and wind up in front of them. (Pros call this "overlapping.") Midfielders will score a lot of your goals, and they should be looking for shots. You'll find that different kids play the position with different temperaments. Some have a bias for the offensive aspect of the position, almost like a forward. Others will play it like a basketball point guard, getting and distributing the ball, preferring to find a teammate they can pass to. And others will play more defensively, making their ability to get back onto defense their highest priority.

Managing your midfielder mix: Of course, you can both choose the mix of natural midfield styles on the field, and you can coach each kid to play the position in today's game according to the needs and opportunities you see. For instance, if I'm concerned about another team scoring a lot of goals against us, I might tell Elliott, normally pretty aggressive at midfield, to pay extra attention to being ready to get back on defense today. Or I might tell the normally point-guard-style player Lauren, "Elliott's going to be the first one back on defense today. So I want you to focus on offense and see if you can find a chance to score a goal."

If our attacking players lose possession of the ball, the midfielders must be the first players to sprint back and begin to help on defense, running to get back between the ball and our goal.

Decisionmaking is really key for midfielders – both what to do with the ball once they gain possession, as we've discussed, and also whether to be in their offensive or defensive mode. Good dribbling skills are a huge advantage, as is being a speedy runner.

I'll also say that at this age, there tends to be less distinction between the roles of forwards and halfbacks, which is okay. But it's good to plant the seed.

Forwards (Offense)

We want our forwards to take the ball up the field (or receive the ball deep in the other team's half of the field) and work it into the other team's goal rectangle. Then we want them to find makeable shots and take them.

The center forward is also known as the striker, in recognition of that player's key role of taking shots on goal. In many of the lineups I gave earlier, there's just a single forward. Obviously, this player occupies the center of the field and looks to camp out in the other team's goal rectangle and shoot. In such a situation, one of the midfielders often plays down one of the wings beside the striker and functions much like a forward for that portion of the attacking phase of the game.

Forwards also have to help on defense, but assuming everyone is doing his or her job, they are going to transition out of the offensive and into the defensive phase of the game only after the midfielders do so. If there is good midfield and fullback coverage of the other team's attack, or if they see the midfielders winning the ball back, we want our forwards to stay, well, forward – in position to counter-attack when we regain possession.

Goalkeeper (Goalie)

Playing this position is so different from all the others that it's almost like playing a different sport. Your goalie can use his hands inside the marked goalie box. He can and often should use his feet and body like a field player. This is a position that makes a lot of kids feel under pressure. Remind them that the whole rest of the team has failed to stop the opponent if the opponent is taking a shot on goal. So your goalie deserves all the praise for saves, but only a small share of the blame if the other team scores. A few principles will give him confidence:

Keep your hands ready: Keeping your goalie's attention on the game can be a big issue. If your offense possesses the ball, the goalie's attention can tend to wander to other games on nearby fields, what's for lunch, or other daydreams. Or he can start to fiddle with his jersey or stick his arms inside the pinnie that designates him as the goalie. Keep an eye out for this from the sideline and admonish, "William, keep your hands ready," or, "William, watch our game!" This focuses him on the flow of the game and gets him to hold up his hands.

Positioning: Though she's allowed to use her hands, we

want the goalie to position her body on the field with a similar strategy to a fullback. Kids' instinct when playing goalie is to stand on the goal line. But this shows the opponent a huge goal, so the only time a goalie should be there is on a penalty kick, when it's required. The rest of the time, we want the goalie at least a few steps in front of the goal, closer to the shooter, making him see a much smaller goal. (The other danger is that the goalie will actually stand behind the goal line, catching the ball only after it's already crossed the line to score a goal.) I find myself constantly reminding kids to "come out of the goal."

Just like a fullback, if a goalie sees a teammate going after the attacker with the ball, the goalie should back up that defender (or, even better, watch as another field player backs up that defender) and wait to see what happens.

However, if the attacker beats all the other defenders, the goalie's job becomes to rush at the attacking player. It goes against kids' every instinct to do that. They just naturally want to hang back and wait for the shot. But rushing the shooter usually makes the shooter miss. It certainly makes for a harder shot, as the goalie's body looms large and eclipses most shooting angles, making the shooter see a small goal. Usually, the ball is kicked and bounces off the goalkeeper's body.

Fielding the ball: When the ball comes to our goalie, the first thing we want him to do is stop its progress toward our net. Sometimes, this means knocking the ball out of the air or diving onto the ground to smother it, and sometimes it's as simple as catching or scooping up a gently struck ball.

However the goalie gains control of the ball, the next thing he needs to do is to end up standing with it hugged to his chest with both arms. By teaching goalies to be strong with the ball like this, we put their focus on securing it. If they're casual about picking it up, they tend to drop it or never get hold of it in the first place, leading to goals.

No punts: With rare exceptions, I forbid my goalies to punt, or drop-kick, the ball. That's because I want our team to keep possession. It is very difficult for a goalie to punt the ball so accurately that it has more than a 50-50 chance of falling to our player. There's a better option than throwing up a jump ball. Instead, I teach my goalkeeper to walk to the front edge of the goalie box and throw or roll it where one of our players can definitely get it first, usually baseball-style. They can use a throw-in motion if they are smaller or not very accurate with the baseball pass. We don't want them to throw it into the middle of the field, but down or toward one of the sidelines.

Much like on throw-ins, this can be a roll right to a teammate's foot. Or, very effectively, it can be throwing the ball over several players' heads into empty space where our player can get to it first. In our season-ending tournament, there was actually a rule against goalie punts past the midfield line. But I had a kid who could easily throw the ball that far, and he put it behind the defense time after time, setting up our midfielders and forwards for scoring chances.

Make sure your goalie doesn't get confused after fielding the ball and set it down on the edge of the goalie box as he would for a goal kick. The other team can come and kick it right into your net for an easy goal. Teach your players to look for this mistake when the other team makes it, though.

Take care to protect the goalkeepers. Obviously, if your goalie is bending down to pick up a ball that the attacking player would really like to kick, that's a vulnerable position. The attacking player is supposed to stop the minute a goalie puts a finger on the ball. If this doesn't happen in the game, make a big deal of it with the referee to protect your player. And coach your offensive players to follow balls all the way in, but to learn to stop the second the goalie lays a finger on it. Praise that level of control in games to help set the example for the other team, as well.

8

Strategies for special situations

Everything so far applies mostly to the usual free-flowing phase of the game. But there are certain moments when special elements of strategy are called for.

Shooting

The first of these I'll discuss is one I touched on earlier when talking about the Shoot-Dribble-Pass decision players must constantly make when they get the ball: When it's time for a player to try to score – to take a shot on goal.

When should I shoot? That's what players need to know. As I said before, it is the right moment to shoot if a player is close enough to the goal, has an unobstructed path to get the ball into it, and thinks she can direct the ball along that path. I distill this advice down to, "When you can see a big goal." That means that some good-size portion of the goal is in your sights unprotected by opposing players. It's bigger when you're reasonably close to it and at a fairly straight angle, and don't have many or any defensive players in your way.

Otherwise, you "see a small goal." Notice that from a sharp angle way off to the side, the goal appears really skinny. That makes it very difficult to hit.

This means that ideally you would like a forward or midfielder to dribble toward the center of the goal as he advances up the field, not way down into the corner where the goal starts to look narrower and narrower. It's a very common tendency at this age for players on the wing to advance too deep into the corner with the ball for no reason when they really need to head for the middle or take the shot from the wing well before the angle narrows so much near the endline.

Every season, I stand kids in front of the goal and have them hold up their hands and measure how much of it they can see. From straight on, it's a nice, big rectangle. Then I move them more toward the sideline, and they see a smaller and smaller trapezoid, and finally down in the corner just the apparent straight line of the superimposed goalposts with no opening.

The point is that on offense, the corners are a place we don't want the ball to stay. If you find yourself there for some reason, your job is to dribble to the middle or to cross the ball into the other team's goal rectangle. If I'm your coach and I see you in the corner or heading toward it, I'm shouting "Middle, middle, middle, middle, middle!" Find a way to get the ball back into the middle, into the other team's goal rectangle. (Of course, this means on defense, we're very happy to shunt the attacking players into the corners.)

The other factor that determines whether a shooter sees a big goal is whether the other team's players put their bodies between her and it. If they leave a lot of space, it's easier to shoot. Many of my team's shots come much farther from the goal than other teams expect – outside the other team's goalie box – when their defenders have left too much space. It can also be very effective for a player to be facing away from the opponent's goal and abruptly turn and shoot. This usually catches the opposing goalie unprepared.

How should I shoot? Well, that depends. There is a great game you can play with kids in practice called "Power and Finesse": Get one of those pop-up goals the size of a doghouse and put it inside the full size goal your team uses in games. Line the players up 25 yards or away so, facing the goal. (This is a line-up-and-take-turns drill that's worth having them endure standing in line). Place yourself to the side of the goals. Call the first kid's name. He runs toward the goal. You roll a ball across the mouth of the big goal and shout, "Power!" The kid blasts the ball into the big net, probably using the laces of his cleat and making the ball leave the ground. Then you quickly cross a second ball and shout, "Fineese!" and the kid has to control the ball precisely to roll it into the smaller goal – a shot that's much less powerful but more accurate. A finesse shot may be struck with the side of the foot, which is shaped like a cradle and offers greater control.

When faced with a chance to score in a game, kids have to make the power vs. finesse decision on their own. Is it to their advantage to blast the ball hard at the goal with a little less accuracy to get it there quickly or to make it hard to block or catch? Or, do they simply need to touch the ball precisely into a small part of the goal that the goalie can't reach (or into an open net)? This practice game is a great lesson, as when a player's facing an undefended net, blasting the ball into the goal only makes scoring less likely – the ball could sail wide or over the crossbar. A point is a point, and there's a lot of deception value in finesse shots, as defenders this age usually expect the ball to be struck hard. Be sure to praise players for finesse shots when that's the right decision and to help them analyze when a finesse shot would've worked better.

Shoot where the goalie isn't. There's a maddening tendency for kids to aim their shots right at the goalkeeper. I think as they try to dial in a target for their shot during the thick of a game, it's just instinctive to choose that human shape, much as they would when passing to a teammate. You have to explain to kids that they want to aim away from the keeper, at an empty portion of the net. This takes lots of practice. The corners are usually a good choice. Teach them to find the corner away from the goalkeeper and try to place the ball there.

Shoot with either foot. Ever see a tennis player run around her backhand? Painful to watch – and ineffective. It's the same way when a soccer player can't shoot with his off foot. When running across the face of the goal toward the left, I probably need to strike the ball with my left foot to shoot on the goal. I'm just at the wrong angle to use my right, unless I can maybe brush it into the net with the outside of my right foot. When I'm new at shooting with my left foot, I'll shoot with less power, but remember that finesse shots are often really effective, so that's fine.

Get kids to practice with their opposite foot in practice (this is hilarious to watch as they first try to figure out how to do it – many actually fall down). Notice when they do shoot with the opposite foot during games and praise them. Point out when an off-foot shot would've been the better decision: "Hey, Miles, that would've been a good one for Mr. Left Foot!" When you're blowing out an opponent, require all your players (or everyone who has already scored) to take shots only with their off foot both to handicap your team and give your players practice in this valuable skill.

Create a great next-to-last touch. When players are dribbling fast down the field on a breakaway, they tend to tap the ball far in front of them. Teach them two things: To use softer touches the whole way to keep it as close to their foot as possible while sprinting down the field. And, most important, to concentrate on the last dribble touch right before the shot – they need to take a very soft touch that puts the ball right where their shooting foot can hit it hard. If they don't focus on this, the ball will roll out of control all the way over the endline without them ever getting a shot. You will see this happen a lot. Tell them that last, soft dribble touch should be like a little pass to their shooting foot.

"One-time" shots: When a player has a chance to shoot a rolling ball accurately without taking a controlling touch first, that's what they should do. That's a great chance to score, and the movement of the ball is so explosive, it's very hard for the opponents to defend. Encourage players to try to touch the ball "one time!" when shooting whenever possible. This could be a loose ball, a pass from a teammate, or a second shot after an initial shot bounces off the goalpost, goalie, or a defender. Have them practice shooting a rolling ball in practice. Obviously, a one-time shot often isn't possible, and players will need a controlling touch or a series of dribble moves before shooting.

Follow the shot. Most kids have the tendency to take a shot and then just stand and watch to see if it goes in. But you want them to "kick it and follow it." To shoot the ball and then run after it, ready to shoot a deflected ball again a second or even third time.

Kickoff

When we get to start at the center circle with control of the ball, you don't want your player to just blast the ball into the other half. The most crucial thing to do is maintain possession for the team while you begin the attack. A slightly sideways, slightly forward tap pass from one front-line player to another is usually the way to start. (If you have a kid with a big foot, it can actually be fun once or twice during the season to have one player tap it over to him and for him to take a shot from midfield.) When the other team's kicking off, get your players to line up on the center circle (this marks the required distance they must stand from the center spot) and remind them to go after the ball, "as soon as they touch it!"

Throw-ins

When we take a throw-in, we usually want to throw it up the sideline toward the other team's end. We definitely don't throw it into our goal rectangle. It's great if there's a way to throw it where our player can get it inside the other team's goal rectangle.

Kids think they should always throw the ball right to a teammate's foot. That can work well, but it's not the only choice. Show them that it's also great to throw it over the teammate's head into empty space where the teammate can run to it first. This gets the ball behind many defenders. It's a big advantage if your kids are able to take your throw-ins really quickly (this is also true for goalie throws). You can catch the other team sleeping and have a better chance of working the ball behind their defense.

When it's the other team's throw, we want to make sure the ball doesn't get behind us and try to steal it if we can.

Corner kicks

On offense, we want our midfielders and forwards to "find big space" in the other team's goalie box, which means unoccupied space where the ball can land in front of them off the corner kick with a chance to put it in. This usually means kids need to stand a little farther back from the goal than they would instinctively choose to leave room for the ball to fall between them and the goal line. Our defenders can sneak way up over the midline of the field so that if the ball squirts out, they can play it back in. Professional teams have elaborate set plays for corner kicks, but at this age, I'd simply improvise.

Goal kicks

Your goalie or your fullback can kick these. Here's another situation where we don't want to blast the ball way up the field unless we can put it into a big space where our player will definitely get it. Otherwise, a nice tap pass to a midfielder. Many leagues back up the other team to the halfway line for goal kicks, and so the defensive key becomes the same as kickoff: "Guys, as soon as they touch it, run get it."

9

Your best tool: The teaching scrimmage

Earlier, I told you practice should mirror the game. I've found that for this age kid, the best way to ensure that happens – and that new skills get integrated into strategic team play – is to let most of practice *be* the game. So I usually spend more than half of each practice in what I think of as a teaching scrimmage.

Agenda for practice

I arrive about 10 minutes before the scheduled start time and greet kids as they arrive, encouraging them to begin with free-form shooting and messing around as other kids arrive. Then, I formally begin practice with the field sprints I described earlier. Then we stretch, and then I demonstrate some skills and concepts and use a few practice activities to emphasize them and let kids try and refine them. There are books and websites full of "drills," so I won't present a stack of them here. You can and should easily make up your own practice activities – just think about how to let kids try out the skill you want to work on, and go for it. Remember that kids need lots of repetition manipulating the ball with their feet and body in ways that are useful in games: Dribbling, passing, and shooting. You can also do tactical drills to help them understand ways to beat a single defender while dribbling alone, or how to beat one defender when they have a teammate to pass to.

How to run a teaching scrimmage

For me, the teaching scrimmage is by far the most useful tool. A scrimmage is just an informal game of soccer. It's great if your roster is big enough to field two teams for a full-field scrimmage. If it's close, don't be afraid to play four (including your strongest player) against five, or six against five to occupy everybody, or to play with small goals and no goalkeepers or whatever you have to do. If you're really shorthanded, you can play offense against the defense. Defense wins when they dribble the ball past midfield or pass to a coach standing across the midfield line.

Like instant replays in real life: Use the freeze-at-the-whistle discipline you've been cultivating to stop the action at important times and talk through what you're seeing and what could be different. You even have the option to make players re-do plays that didn't turn out the way they should've to show players how following your instructions will produce a better result.

Get out there with them. You can even involve yourself in the play, dribbling or passing to show kids how you want it done. (If you join them on the field, be very careful not to collide with, step on, or fall onto these much smaller players.) As I mentioned earlier, you'll often simply freeze play to get players to examine where they are on the field and then make an adjustment.

Teaching scrimmages are your chance to coach in the

middle of the field as the kids play. You can go up to individual players for private conversations about how they can better do their jobs or walk them through where you want them to position themselves while play is going on. Teaching scrimmages are great for introducing players to new positions they haven't played much. (Incidentally, I usually start new players on defense, then show them midfield, then offense, and only after all of that, goalie.) If you have assistant coaches, one of you can coach the overall game and the others can go around to tutor individual players. It can also be good to switch players among positions. If you're running your midfielders really hard, switch them to defense for new skills and less running.

Push the pace. I do seek to minimize the pauses I introduce to teaching scrimmages, and also to make up for them by pushing the pace of scrimmages faster than a typical game pace. So sometimes I have us do corner kicks, throw-ins, and goal kicks just like a game, but often I just keep a spare ball with me, and if the ball goes far out of play, I toss or punt it up in the air and shout, "New ball! Play!" Players get to practice controlling a loose ball – the type of loose ball that often results from our opponents' goalie punts. If younger siblings are on the sidelines for practice, they often love the job of retrieving errant balls and making sure you always have a spare in hand.

I also tell the players not to consider the ball out of bounds unless I whistle it, and I let them stretch the edges of the field a quite a bit to minimize the stoppages. This is good practice for the fact that the ball is not out in a game until the ref says, and that if you stop playing before that, you give the other team an advantage.

This intensive pace in teaching scrimmages also helps players improve their physical conditioning and teaches them to be alert for anything to happen. Don't forget to whistle water breaks, particularly on hot days. And tell every child to take a drink of water at every break.

One other tip: These are so much fun that you have to remember to keep track of the time, because it's easy to get caught up and let practice run long, which upsets your players' parents.

Circle time

You can end practice with circle time – and I have it after every game to debrief, too. I hold it over by the sideline where all the parents have been watching. I want them to overhear what I'm emphasizing with the kids. I remind the kids what they learned, that they got great exercise. I take any questions the kids have, and I may tell them a couple of things they can think about or practice at home on their own or with their siblings or parent.

I re-emphasize any upcoming logistical information, such as the the time and field of our upcoming game or deviations from the normal practice schedule.

10

Take it one thing at a time

I've given you a lot of ideas, so one final reminder: You have to roll these concepts out very gradually over the course of a season. If you try to do them all at once, you'll make things too complicated too quickly, just like those ex-elite college players who coach.

In fact, let me caution that there's way too much here for beginner teams to take on in a single soccer season. Just begin with the first one or two ideas, and work on those until your team gets these down. Then add the next right thing. If you have a returning core group of kids from season to season, you can catch the newcomers up on what the team mostly knows, and then you can to add the next concept.

Even if you do this at just the right pace, periodically you will have to remind the kids of earlier principles they had mastered. It may seem frustrating for a awhile, but then one day, you'll be coaching a game, and you'll realize you haven't shouted an instruction for several minutes, and they'll just be playing beautifully because they practiced it all enough to internalize it. And that's a beautiful thing to see.

So, be patient, be positive, and enjoy yourself and the kids.

Thanks for deciding to coach elementary soccer – I hope you and your team find fun and success this season.

Appendix

Team management

Team communication

Families have busy schedules and lots of demands on their attention. The best thing you can do is establish good communication and clear expectations right away. Then you have to keep working to listen and observe and answer people's questions. If you have a spouse or partner on the sidelines, ask him or her for intel.

I think the best way to summarize how to manage the team is to share with you the email I send out as soon as the league provides my roster at the beginning of the season. It's long! You have my permission to use the text of this email as-is or to adapt it:

Hello, U8 TUSA families.

I'm Bryan Gilmer, Quinn's dad, volunteer head coach of our team. I'm writing to welcome a few of you back from our great team from last year and to welcome many of you for the first time. I'm writing to say hi to you all, let you know how excited I am about the season, and give you important information:

Practices start NEXT WEEK on Monday, Aug. 25: It's on Monday and Wednesday evenings at Holt Fields, 98 Hedgerow Pl, Durham, NC (way back behind the N. Roxboro Kroger shopping center in the Old Farm neighborhood -- this is NOT Holt Elementary), from 6-7:15 pm. It can be very tricky to find for the first time. Here's a link to a map: http://tinyurl.com/holtfields

Monday evening practices will be skills training sessions by paid TUSA staff coaches. On those nights, our team will work out with a larger group of TUSA players, including some older players. These sessions really helped our players build their ball handling skills last year. On Wednesdays, we'll work out as just our team. These are the nights I will focus on applying the skills we each have to a common team strategy. You must stay with your child during practices or leave another responsible adult there with him/her instead of dropping your child off. Both Monday and Wednesday night practices are mandatory.

Here's our roster (subject to some changes as the league finalizes things): *[names deleted for confidentiality]*

Philosophy: We play in a competitive league, and I want our team to succeed. However, at this age in this developmental league, true success means developing as players. So, your child will very likely play all of the positions in the lineup during the season at least a little. We don't want to pigeonhole players into a single position this young. I do think we will again win a fair number of games (last season with a different lineup, we were actually undefeated until losing in the season-end tournament championship game), and I want us to. More important is that they have a great time, run hard, and exercise. My son, Quinn, certainly needs the field time after all the desk time he's getting in second grade. Help me to keep the sideline commentary positive and encouraging. Reinforce the messages I and our other coaches are sending. Congratulate the other team when they play well. Be kind and even gracious to the (mostly teenage) referees. Let's model great sportsmanship for the kids and for the parents on the other team.

COACHING ELEMENTARY SOCCER

Uniforms and gear: Each player will receive a jersey, shorts, socks, and a practice shirt. I will distribute the items as soon as they arrive, but I don't have them yet. Your child must wear cleats in this league, as some fields get soupy and the extra traction prevents sliding down. Please wear comfortable shorts and TUSA practice T-shirts to practice once you have them. Shin guards covered by soccer socks are mandatory at all practices and games. If your child does not have them, he/she will not be able to participate that day, as this is a true safety issue.

Your child needs a size 4 soccer ball and must bring it to each practice. Please write the child's name and your cell number on the ball in Sharpie so it can be returned to you if lost. Please no wristwatches, jewelry, etc. while playing. Put long hair up in braids, ponytail or secure headband. Please bring plenty of water for your child to drink. Most of the kids have a sports bottle with their name on it, and you can refill it with cool (but not frigid) tap water before each practice and game.

Draconian snack policy: A quick word on my snack policy, which is probably a little more strict than what you're used to. I hope it doesn't bother anyone. Obviously, you can feed your own child anything you decide. But when it is your family's turn to feed all the kids by bringing team snacks, I ask that we provide no drink (they can drink from the water bottle they brought). Please no processed/sugary snacks. Preferred options are whole or simply sliced fruit – such as a banana, orange, apple, pear, grapes, blueberries – or vegetables – carrot sticks or celery sticks in a cup with a little ranch at the bottom.

Please no cookies, chips, Capri Sun, sports drinks, or even fruit juice boxes. A granola bar or yogurt tube might slide by, as well. Research shows that healthy kids this age need plenty of water when exercising at the intensity we will, and this policy is intended to help them gain eating habits that don't undo all the exercise they just did. If we play more than one game on the same day, then chocolate milk and sports drinks between games are good. Please let me know if you would be willing to compile and manage the team snack list.

BRYAN GILMER

I'm really excited for the season, looking forward to meeting you all, and here for any questions you might have. My cell number is 919-XXX-YYYY. Don't hesitate to reach out if you have a question or want to tell me something about your child that might help me coach him or her.

Best wishes,
Coach Bryan

During the season, I just reply-all to that first email to announce that practice is rained out, explain where this weekend's game will be played, talk about what we're working on in practice, or whatever.

Why shin guards: Most leagues require them, and many referees check to make sure kids are wearing them before kickoff. Regardless, kids need them. Kids are out there kicking at the ball, and they will end up kicking shins. The Velcro strap kind need to be worn underneath long soccer socks to stay in place, but inevitably some kid wants to come to practice with them strapped onto his bare legs.

Why cleats: I advise against cleats for preschoolers, but elementary kids definitely need them both in practice and in games, and your league may require them. They're moving fast enough now to need the extra traction, particularly when the field is wet. Cleats are designed to create smooth kicking surfaces that make it easier to control the ball.

Sandals, dress shoes and Crocs-style shoes all make for poor protection, poor ball control, or poor traction. Don't let kids wear them. Also don't allow cleats with metal or triangular plastic spikes, which can injure other players. Round or elongated cleat nubs are correct for soccer.

Go for the combo: A chain sporting goods store near us usually offers a shin guards/ball/cleats combo pack for about $30 when the season is starting, so it's not very expensive for kids to outfit themselves correctly.

Why the Draconian snack policy: It's a big tradition in many leagues and maybe across America for parents to take turns bringing an after-game snack. But too many times since I've been coaching, this is a giant dose of sugar.

People buy those kid drinks in the silver pouches with the tiny straw because they're cheap and portable. I put up with this until one day when a mom brought the punch pouches plus little packages with chocolate cookies in one end and a sugar paste like sandwich cookie filling in a tub-like compartment at the other end.

Why water to drink: We're supposed to be teaching kids healthy habits, like getting frequent exercise. What a child who has exercised needs is plenty of water, and not sugar water (which is mostly what even fruit juice is).

I decided to buy a cylindrical drinking water cooler and bring it full to each game and practice to make it easy for families. (I also ask each family to bring a reusable cup or water bottle, which the child can refill from the cooler. I always bring a few extra cups, too, as some kid's parent inevitably forgets.

What you need, Coach

Your league may supply some or all of these:

- **Sneakers, not cleats**. The risk of you stepping on a child's foot in cleats while practicing with them is an unacceptable risk. Yes, the kids will step on your feet with their cleats, and it hurts – but at least they weigh 1/3 as much as you.
- **A whistle** (about a dollar at any discount store)
- **Two or three extra soccer balls** for certain practice games and to share with kids who forget to bring a ball.
- **Practice pinnies**, little colored tank-top overshirts that are a couple bucks apiece you can let the kids wear in practice to group them into teams. You can use one to designate your goalie during games.
- **Little plastic orange cones,** not the beefy ones they

put near potholes, but the flatter ones about the size of a saucer or compact disc that you can use to mark out areas on the field in practice. In fact, you could use unwanted CDs or beanbags.
- **Sports ball inflation pump:** These are little hand pumps with a short hose and an inflator needle. Many families don't have one at home. You can bring it to practice and make sure the balls are not over- or under-inflated – and if you don't, they will be.
- **A mesh bag** to keep it all in.
- **A drinking water cooler with push-button spout** and some plastic cups. You don't need the big ones like they pour onto the heads of coaches. The one I have is a 2-gallon size, and I fill it about two-thirds full with a little bit of ice. It's much more manageable to carry from the car to the sideline.

Involve the other parents

The other parents on your team are sitting there on the sidelines with very little to do. Some of them will have smaller children to manage (though you can still recruit one of those parents to sign each family up for a game day to provide the snack).

Most other parents are very happy to help and to come out onto the field and play with you and the kids during practice. It's a blast to have a physician in his scrubs and a mom in her business suit running around with the kids.

Decide exactly what you would like for them to do, and then just ask. If another parent starts trying to take over, just have a friendly conversation telling them you've got a progression in mind for the practice.

When you find a parent you work well with, ceremoniously designate her as your official assistant coach (if your league hasn't already assigned you one). This way, if you need to go out of town on game day or practice night, you have someone ready to fill in.

Season-end team party

One of my favorite parts of each season is the team party. I usually schedule this for the same evening as our usual practice day right after the season ends. People have the slot blocked out on their weekly calendars already, so most families can easily make it. If you don't want to host this at your own house, start asking around to find a family on your team that will. You can make it a potluck or get someone to cook dinner.

It's amazing that it took so long to strike me, but this season, I had our party at a city park where there was a grassy area and the kids could play soccer after eating pizza, and they loved it.

I like to have a little season-ending ceremony and say something nice about each child in front of all the other kids and parents.

I recommend you start planning the team party as the season opens – or get your snack list manager to do so.

ABOUT THE AUTHOR

Bryan Gilmer has made his living as a writer for more than 20 years, working first as a newspaper reporter in Greenville, South Carolina, before moving on to Florida's largest newspaper, the *St. Petersburg Times*, now the *Tampa Bay Times*. Now he works as the director of marketing and development for a nonprofit homeless shelter. He also writes crime novels for an adult audience. They include **Kill the Story**, a mystery, and the thrillers **Felonious Jazz** and **Record of Wrongs**, both available on Amazon.com and Kindle.

E-mail Bryan at bryan@bryangilmer.com; visit his website at BryanGilmer.com; subscribe to his page on Facebook; or follow him on Twitter: @BryanGilmer.

www.ingramcontent.com/pod-product-compliance
Lightning Source LLC
Chambersburg PA
CBHW061341040426
42444CB00011B/3027